THE RAPTURE OF THE SAINTS

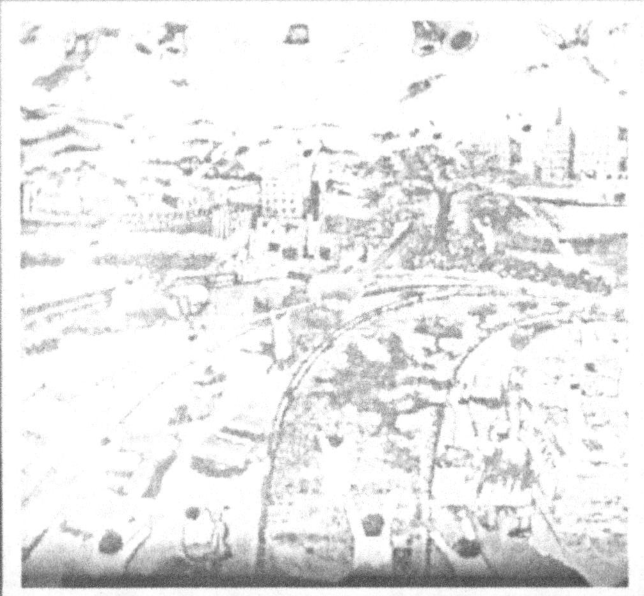

THE SUPERNATURAL FLIGHT TO MEET JESUS IN THE AIR

S.O.A ADEDIRAN.

THE RAPTURE OF THE SAINTS

THE SUPERNATURAL FLIGHT TO MEET JESUS IN THE AIR

S.O.A. ADEDIRAN

Published by:
The Way of Truth Mission (WATRUM)
No. 58, Fehinti-Oluwa Qtrs.,
P.O. Box 111, Kabba, Kogi State, Nigeria.
e-mail:
thewayoftruthmission@gmail.com
+2348032200580, +2347082926262
+2344805891563

ISBN: 978-978-967-581-4

All scripture quotations are from King James Version of the Holy Bible unless otherwise indicated.

Designed & Printed by:
Babs Ventures,
Shop 19/20 Old Minna Park, Behind ECWA Church, Suleja, Niger State.
Tel: 08035911252, 08053919762

CONTENTS

ACKNOWLEDGEMENTS

I give all glory, honour and adoration to the coming King that died on the cross to save me from the wrath to come. I also give my heartfelt appreciation to my loving wife for perusing through the manuscript and for her useful contributions. I am highly indebted to my dear mother who served as an angel of God in nursing me during the challenges of my infancy and childhood years, and for being observant that I would be a minister of God

I am deeply grateful to a resilient soldier of Christ, late Evangelist M.A. Awuto who God used to tutor my life for a period of twelve years. I have a great delight to express my profound gratitude to my first Pastor and G.O Apostle P.A. Forward whose words and prayer God has used to encourage me in the Ministry. I also thank my Pastor, Sam Anjorin who searched for vital information on the internet to update events I refer to in this book and my son in the Lord, David Precious who laboured constantly in preparing the manuscript.

My unreserved gratitude goes to my daughter and lecturer Mrs. Naomi Favour Ayeni for editing the manuscript.

I will not fail to thank Pastor Adeleye Ibimode and Engr. Moses Olusegun for their silent labour in making this book a reality. I love to sincerely thank Pastor Dave Dan for his constant fatherly pieces of advice. I also acknowledge my daddy, Rev. J.P Waiye for writing the foreword to this book. I will not fail to appreciate Engr. Paul Omojadi who was the messenger God sent to preach on rapture at my conversion and Bishop A.J. Love who did the follow-up.

I equally appreciate my daughter, Inioluwa Winner Adediran, whose constant dream on the imminence of the rapture hastened me up in the writing of this book. I want to express my unreserved gratitude to all the Pastors and Co-labourers in the vineyard of God for their silent labour and all the saints that have contributed to the success of this book. The Lord will reward all your labour of love in Jesus name. Amen.

DEDICATION

This book is dedicated to the Bridegroom Who cleanses and sanctifies His Brides with His own blood to make them fit for the rapture. And to Pastor W.F. Kumuyi of Deeper Christian Life Ministry, whose unwavering stand for holiness has encouraged me not to sway from the way of truth.

PREFACE

When Jesus Christ our Master and Lord came to the world over two thousand years ago, He sent His disciples to the neighbouring villages to preach on a message ***the kingdom of heaven is at hand,*** Matthew 10:7. Before Jesus began His public ministry, John the Baptist preached the same message in the wilderness of Judea saying, ***Repent ye for the kingdom of heaven is at hand.*** (Matthew 3:2).

If it was so important to warn people to prepare for the kingdom of God at that time, then, it is imperative and of great necessity to preach it with urgency in our generation to whom the end of the world is coming.

It was a message of rapture that was preached to me when I gave my life to Jesus on 11th December, 1987. Since then, my heart has been longing for that glorious day that my Lord will appear in the sky. Moreover, I have a keen interest in studying to know when and how the rapture will take place. I prepared the first comprehensive teaching on it, when I had the privilege to teach on campus fellowship in 1997. I gave full attention to the teaching in the Church I pastored in 1998 and also preached on it everywhere the Lord gave me the privilege. As the years rolled by, the Lord impressed it on my heart to put it in writing in order to reach areas I could not go.

Rapture is a timely message. The prophecies about it are fulfilled and are being fulfilled in our very eyes. The present time in the programme of God is clearly explained in this book. Every wise Christian that reads will see how urgent it is to prepare for the first and the last flights – the rapture of the saints. I pray God will rekindle the fire of revival in you to prepare for the glorious rapture as you read this book in Jesus name.

Your servant in Christ,

Sam Adediran
19th June, 2018.

FOREWORD

The Rapture Of The Saints

We live in an era when the message about the rapture and the second coming of Christ is fast fading away. When I became born again in the late 70s, the reason for becoming a Christian and for going to church was the kingdom of God. More than seventy percent of the messages you hear in the church then were about getting ready for the rapture. But today, the focus has drastically changed to the detriment of the church. The reasons for going to church today are no longer for the kingdom of God nor for preparation for the rapture, but for earthly and material gains.

I had the privilege of ministering in a PFN program some time ago in Lagos,

Nigeria, and I told them that the church no longer seeks God today, the church seeks things. I told them that the major problem in the church today is that there is no seeking of the Lord anymore. Many church members today know nothing about the rapture. Since their Pastors had never said anything about it.

Although there are so many prayer houses and mountains everywhere today, there is less of seeking the Lord and the kingdom of God. Rather than seeking the Lord, people seek things. Sadly enough, church leaders have left the business of seeking the Lord for seeking things. When leaders are things seekers, what do you expect from the followers? Ministers are actually leading people to seek things rather than to seek God.

We now believe that ministry success is all about the things we possess. The kind of building you worship in or live in, the kind of car you drive, how many countries of the world you have visited, fame, popularity etc. Because these are the things we seek rather than seeking the Lord and preparing members for the rapture, we live in gigantic buildings but not in God's presence. We know America and all of Europe but we don't know the secret place of the most high. We drive the best cars around but are not driven by the Holy Spirit and His purpose. You are known all over the world, but heaven does not know you. The rapture and second coming of Christ is not in your agenda. What kind of ministry is that? Just food and belly?

Thank God for a man of God like Pastor Adediran who has taken it upon himself to write this timely book on this all important subject of the rapture of the saints. Missing the rapture is the greatest of all misses in life. Those who miss the rapture are doomed!

Although there are various teachings and notions about the rapture, what is most important, as far as I am concerned, is for one to be ready when Jesus comes for His saints. And the only way to be ready and not be left behind is to, like Enoch, please God with your life and your lifestyle. Even if you don't know much theology about the rapture, it suffices to know that if you live a life that pleases God, you will not miss the rapture. The most important thing about the rapture is that you don't miss it.

The book is so enlightening and challenging. I have no hesitation recommending it to everyone who does not want the coming of the Lord to meet him unawares. By all means, make sure you don't miss the rapture. May the grace of God be sufficient for you in Jesus name.

Rev. Waiye Jethro Prince
General
Overseer, Revival
Hour Ministries
Intl. LAGOS.

INTRODUCTION

The hope of the Church is the rapture. Every believer in Christ that misses the rapture will have to face the wrath of the antichrist in the seven years of untold torture and unbearable suffering coming on the inhabitants of the world. This is called the great tribulation. The rapture will mark the beginning of the great tribulation. Though the term Rapture is not in the Bible, the theory is based on the scripture.

Then shall two be in the field; the one shall be taken, and the other left. Two women shall be grinding at the mill; the one shall be taken, and the other left. Matthew 24:40,41. ***For the Lord himself shall descend from heaven with a shout, with the voice of the archangel, and with the trump of God: and the dead in Christ shall rise first: Then we which are alive and remain shall be caught up together with them in the clouds, to meet the Lord in the air: and so shall we ever be with the Lord.*** 1 Thessalonians 4:16, 17.

The rapture is the first phase of the second coming of Jesus Christ to the earth. The second coming of Christ is prophesied in the Bible. It is mentioned 318 times in the New Testament. The Lord Jesus, the angels, the Apostles and Disciples confirmed it. It was also predicted in the Old Testament. Therefore, the Saints in Christ should be ready for the second coming of Christ. The fulfillment of the prophecy of His first coming is an evidence that the prophecy of His second coming will certainly be fulfilled. Although many people were aware of the prophecy of His first coming yet it took them unawares.

The wise men from the East saw His sign and came to pay homage in Jerusalem where Christ was born but the people of Jerusalem with their priests were in the dark as to whether Christ the Saviour had been born or not. Therefore, the saints in Christ must be aware and be prepared lest the first phase of His second coming (The Rapture) meet them unprepared. The rapture is meant to take the glorious church of Christ from earth to meet the Lord in the air.

For our conversation is in heaven; from whence also we look for the Saviour, the Lord Jesus Christ. *Philippians 3:20.*

CHAPTER 1

THE DEFINITION AND THE PURPOSE OF THE RAPTURE

The meaning of rapture is derived from the Latin word rapturo meaning caught up. In Christian circle, it means to be caught up to meet the Lord in the air. It can also be defined

as the supernatural flight of the believers in Christ to meet the Lord in the air. In a moment, in the twinkling of an eye, at the last trump, the dead in Christ shall rise and the believers in Christ shall be caught up to meet the Lord in the cloud. It should not be an incredible matter for God to Change the body or translate it from one state to another.

But someone may ask, How will the dead be brought back to life again?

What kind of bodies will they have? What a foolish question! You will find the answer in your own garden! When you put a seed into the ground it doesn't grow into a plant unless it dies first. And when the green shoot comes up out of the seed, it is very different from the seed you first planted. For all you put into the ground is a dry little seed of wheat or whatever it is you are planting, then God gives it a beautiful new body-just the kind he wants it to have; a different kind of plant grows from each kind of seed, 1 Corinthians 15:35-38. TLB *Now this I say, brethren, that flesh and blood cannot inherit the kingdom of God; neither doth corruption inherit incorruption. Behold, I shew you a mystery; We shall not all sleep, but we shall all be changed, In a moment, in the twinkling of an eye, at the last trump: for the trumpet shall sound, and the dead shall be raised incorruptible, and we shall be*

changed. 1 Corinthians 15:50-52

This present mortal [corruptible] body is subject to decay and is bound under the law of gravity. The new, incorruptible body at rapture will defile the law of gravity. It is not subject to the law of gravity because the saints that will be rapturable must have overcome the law of sin (sinful nature) in their lifetime.

For I delight in the law of God after the inward man, but I see another law in my members, warring against the law of my mind, and bringing me into captivity to the law of sin which is in my members." Romans 7:22, 23

Therefore, the law of gravity can only exercise its power over people that are conquered by the natural law of sin. It will hold them to the earth and any human effort to go further will be futile. It will not give sinners passage to heaven. However, the law of gravity will lose power over the saints at rapture. The saints will yell at it as they have a glorious passage to meet the Lord in the cloud. What a veneration of great honor that awaits the saints of Christ at the rapture!

In addition, the resurrection of our body is described by the seeds we plant. They have life in their cotyledon when planted. Whenever they are planted, each of them dies and then brings forth another different body that is fresh and totally different from the seeds that were planted. If God gives each kind of seed its own body, how should we think it incredible for God to give an immortal body to replace the mortal body at resurrection? Though the natural body is subject to corruption (decay), at resurrection we shall be raised with supernatural bodies that cannot decay, or have any blemish and that cannot be subject to any infirmity.

As the plants spring forth with glorious bodies that are better than the seeds, so also, the believers in Christ will be raised with bodies that are greater in glory at resurrection. This glorious body cannot be depressed or suffer from any blemish. I may not be able to describe vividly the way we shall be, but I know that ***"...when He shall appear, we shall be like Him..."*** 1John 3:2

Undoubtedly, God has revealed His power to us in the past on the possibility of the rapture. We have records of men that went to heaven by rapture and not through death. In the antediluvian age, Enoch was raptured,

By faith Enoch was translated that he should not see death; and was not found, because God had translated him: for before his translation he had this testimony, that he pleased God. Hebrews 11:5.

Before Enoch could be translated, he had a testimony among men and in the sight of God that he pleased God. It is important to know that God does not translate people by chance or by luck. Your life must first please God. Pleasing God means to live for God's pleasure and not your own. It is a life that God derives joy in. It is a life that honors God, irrespective of human oppositions or opinions. Hence, God took Enoch out of his wicked generation to join Him in heaven. He went to heaven without passing through the gate of death. While death would be furiously gazing at him in horror, he mocked and taunted death as he followed God into the entrance of the pearly gate of heaven. Hallelujah! He was the first to go to heaven by rapture. God will also preserve you for His heavenly kingdom if your life is pleasing unto him and if you walk with Him consistently without wavering. Can you say your life is pleasing unto God?

Elijah also went on rapture at the period of the kings while our Lord Jesus also was caught up in the air after His resurrection.

And it came to pass, as they still went on, and talked, that, behold, there appeared a chariot of fire, and horses of fire, and parted them both asunder; and Elijah went up by a whirlwind into heaven. 2 Kings 2:11. ***"And when he had spoken these things, while they beheld, he was taken up; and a cloud received him out***

of their sight .And while they looked stedfastly toward heaven as he went up, behold, two men stood by them in white apparel; Which also said, Ye men of Galilee, why stand ye gazing up into heaven? This same Jesus, which is taken up from you into heaven, shall so come in like manner as ye have seen him go into heaven. Acts 1:9-11.

One of the groups of people that will go on rapture are the children that have not reached the age of accountability.

And they brought unto him also infants, that he would touch them: but when his disciples saw it, they rebuked them. But Jesus called them unto him, and said, suffer little children to come unto me, and forbid them not: for of such is the kingdom of God. Verily I say unto you, whosoever shall not receive the kingdom of God as a little child shall in no wise enter therein. Luke 18:15-17.

The journey of the children of Israel to the promised land is a good example. Those that were already adults when they left Egypt, God destroyed them in the wilderness for their unbelief and sins, except Caleb and Joshua that entered the Promised Land with the children.

Surely none of the men that came up out of Egypt, from twenty years old and upward, shall see the land which I sware unto Abraham, unto Isaac, and unto Jacob; because they have not wholly followed me: Save Caleb the son of Jephunneh the Kenezite, and Joshua the son of Nun: for they have wholly followed the LORD. Numbers 32:11-12.

Moreover your little ones, which ye said should be a prey, and your children, which in that day had no knowledge between good and evil, they shall go in thither, and unto them will I give it, and they shall possess it. Deuteronomy 1:39.

Some parents who are too indulgent towards their children, placing them above their love for God will see their children disappear in their very eyes while they will be left behind. However, the chance of making the rapture is higher for the children whose parents are saved.

"For the unbelieving husband is sanctified by the wife, and the unbelieving wife is sanctified by the husband: else were your children unclean; but now are they holy. 1 Corinthians 7:14.

Hence, if one of them is saved, it guarantees the holiness of their children that have not reached the age of accountability.

There are three schools of thought on the issue of the rapture. The first believes the rapture would take place after the great tribulation and are called post-tribulation believers. They hold to Matthew 24:29, 30.

Immediately after the tribulation of those days shall the sun be darkened, and the moon shall not give her light, and the stars shall fall from heaven, and the powers of the heavens shall be shaken: And then shall appear the sign of the Son of man in heaven: and then shall all the tribes of the earth mourn, and they shall see the son of man, coming in the clouds of heaven with power and great glory.

Invariably, the second school of thought believes the rapture would take place at the middle of great tribulation and are called Mid-great tribulation believers, they also hold to 2 Thessalonians 2:3

"Let no man deceive you by any means: for that day shall not come, except there come a falling away first, and that man of sin be revealed, the son of perdition.

THE CLEAR EVIDENCES OF CHRIST RETURN BEFORE THE GREAT TRIBULATION.

The third school of thought believes the rapture would take place before the great tribulation and are called pre-great tribulation believers. The scripture is explicitly clear on the fact that the rapture will precede the great tribulation. Some bible scholars that could not differentiate the second advent of Christ from the rapture mix it up. They don't understand the difference between the tribulation the Church will go through and the great tribulation (period of God's wrath on the unbelievers after the rapture).

1. *Whereas, the bible teaches that believers are not appointed to*

wrath.

For God hath not appointed us to wrath, but to obtain salvation by our Lord Jesus Christ. 1 Thessalonians 5:9.

2. *Though the early Church went through Tribulation, They Did not go through the Great Tribulation. Revelation 2:10, 2Timothy 3:12.*

Because thou hast kept the word of my Patience, I also will keep thee from the hour of temptation, which shall come upon all the world, to try them that dwell upon the earth. Revelation 3:10

3. *AS IT WAS IN THE DAYS OF NOAH, LOT AND ENOCH who escaped before God's wrath descended, so shall the coming of Christ be.*

The angel said to Lot, ***Escape for thy life, look not behind thee, neither stay thou in all the plain, escape to the mountain, lest thou be consumed Haste thee escape thither for I CANNOT DO ANY THING TILL THOU BE COME THITHER*** Genesis 19:17-22.

likewise also as it was in the days of lot; the same day that Lot went out of Sodom, it rained fire and brimstone from heaven and destroyed them all. Even thus shall it be in the day when the son of man is revealed. Luke 17:26-30.

4. The great tribulation is called the time of Jacob's trouble

connected to Israel.

Alas! for that day is great, so that none is like it: it is even the time Jacob's trouble; but he shall be saved out of it. *Jeremiah 30:7. Whereas, the church is under the time of grace.*

Verily, verily, I say unto you, He that heareth my word, and believeth on him that sent me, hath everlasting life, and shall not come into condemnation; but is passed from death unto life. John 5:24

5. The saints in Christ shall appear with Christ at His second advent. **when Christ, who is our life, shall appear, then shall ye also appear with him in glory.** Colossian 3:4.

That shows we must have gone on

rapture before then.

6. The marriage supper is in heaven and Christ is to return with the glorified saints. Revelation 19:4-14.

   And Enoch also, the seventh from Adam, prophesied of these, saying, Behold, the Lord cometh with ten thousands of his saints. Jude 1:14.

7. I will show you things which must be hereafter (Rev.4:1) is evidence because from Revelation chapter four (4) upward are the events that will take place after the church. Hence, the church would have been taken up; only those that are spouted out will be left here for judgment. Revelation 3:16.

   Verily, verily, I say unto you, he that heareth my word, and believeth on

> **him that sent me, hath everlasting life, and shall not come into condemnation; but is passed from death unto life.** John 5:24

Therefore, it is obvious that God would have taken His own elect out of the world before the great tribulation. God cannot release His wrath until He has taken His church out of the world. Meanwhile, the church in this context is not referring to the local church but the universal church of Christ in which all genuine believers in Christ are partakers.

Invariably, the purpose of the rapture that you see below makes it clear that the church will not take part in the great tribulation.

One of the reasons for the rapture is the resurrection of the dead in Christ. Note the dead in Christ,

The Lord himself shall descend from heaven, with a shout, and the dead in Christ shall rise first. 1 Thessalonians 4:16.

This refers to all the believers in Christ who have slept in the Lord as at the time the rapture will take place on earth. It begins with the first man who died in Christ. The penitent malefactor that obtained mercy at his last hour when he was hanged beside Jesus Christ on the cross.

And Jesus said unto him, Verily I say unto thee, To day shalt thou be with me in paradise. Luke 23:43. 1 Cor 15:21-23; 57-58. 1 Cor 15:51-58, Phil 3:20,

2 Cor 5:1-8, 2 Thess 2:1, 7, 8, Luke 21:34-36 and

1 Thess 4:13-17. Other reasons are:

To keep the saints away from the wrath of the antichrist. Before the anger of God is released upon the ungodly, He will call His representatives that are upon the earth. Believers are not appointed to wrath. So God would have taken His elect out of the world before the great tribulation transpires on earth.

For God hath not appointed us to wrath, but to obtain salvation by our Lord Jesus Christ. 1 Thessalonians 5:9. To give reward to the saints who have laboured faithfully in the vineyard of God.

Henceforth there is laid up for me a crown of righteousness, which the Lord, the righteous judge, shall give me at that day: and not to me only, but unto all them also that love his appearing. 2 Timothy 4:8.

Every mans work shall be made manifest: for the day shall declare it, because it shall be revealed by fire; and the fire shall try every mans work of what sort it is. If any mans work abide which he hath built thereupon, he shall receive a reward. If any mans work shall be burned, he shall suffer loss: but he himself shall be saved; yet so as by fire. 1 Corinthians 3:13-15.

This will take place at Bema (the judgment seat of Christ). There the work of every believer will be tested by fire. If anyone suffers loss, yet shall be saved as one who passed through fire.

And, behold, I come quickly; and my reward is with me, to give every man according as his work shall be. Revelation 22:12.

The rapture is also meant to gather the saints in Christ at the marriage supper of the lamb.

And I heard as it were the voice of a great multitude, and as the voice of many waters, and as the voice of mighty thunderings, saying, Alleluia: for the Lord God omnipotent reigneth. Let us be glad and rejoice, and give honour to him: for the marriage of the Lamb is come, and his wife hath made herself ready. And to her was granted that she should be arrayed in fine linen, clean and white: for the fine linen is the righteousness of saints. And he saith unto me, Write, Blessed are they which are called unto the marriage supper of the Lamb. And he saith unto me, These are the true sayings of God. Revelation 19:6-9.

It is going to be a glorious day for all that will be at the glorious wedding of the lamb. The joy of the brides will know no bounds. Friends, are you ready for that day of joy? Is your garment pure? Is it not already stained with iniquities? Maybe you don't even have the white garment, which is the righteousness of the saints.

And when the king came to see the guests, he saw there a man which had not on a wedding garment: And he saith unto him, Friend, how camest thou in hither not having a wedding garment? And he was speechless. Matthew 22:11-12.

It was through religion you came into the fold, if you have not repented of your sins, with a strong decision to forsake them and receive Jesus as your Lord and Saviour, the Master will ask where you passed through. John 10:1. Friend, how did you come into the fold? Is it not the religion of your parents that brought you in? Or you were invited to a church and in sincerity of your heart, you became a member of the church. That is why you are not free from sin. If you have passed through the right door (Jesus Christ), He would have removed your filthy garment from you and clothed you with the white wedding garment. If you profess to be a Christian and you are living in sin, you did not pass through the right door. This is because in Christ, there is no sin.

And ye know that he was manifested to take away our sins; and in him is no sin. Whosoever abideth in him sinneth not: whosoever sinneth hath not seen him, neither known him. 1 John 3:5-6.

You can receive your wedding garment today by confessing your sins to God and receive Jesus as your Lord and personal Saviour.

CHAPTER 2

THE DIFFERENCES BETWEEN THE RAPTURE AND THE SECOND ADVENT

A vivid study of the Bible clearly reveals that there are two great events in the second coming of our Lord Jesus Christ. The first event is the Supernatural flight of the purified believers in Christ to heaven while the second event is the second advent of Christ to this world to reign for one thousand years. There are interval of seven years between the rapture and the second advent of Christ. It is imperative to know the differences between the rapture and the Second Advent lest we begin to mix them up. The understanding of this will help us know and differentiate the scripture referring to the rapture from the one talking about the Second

Advent of Christ. The rapture marks the beginning of seven years of great tribulation on earth while the second advent of Christ marks the beginning of a thousand year-reign of Christ on earth.

And I saw thrones, and they sat upon them, and judgment was given unto them: and I saw the souls of them that were beheaded for the witness of Jesus, and for the word of God, and which had not worshiped the beast, neither his image, neither had received his mark upon their foreheads, or in their hands; and they lived and reigned with Christ a thousand years. Revelation 20:4.

At this supernatural flight, the Holy Spirit will go with the believers to heaven.

For the mystery of iniquity doth already work: only he who now letteth will let, until he be taken out of the way. And then shall that wicked be revealed, whom the Lord shall consume with the spirit of his mouth, and shall destroy with the brightness of his coming. 2 Thessalonians 2:7, 8.

Though many horrible and unimaginable sins are already introduced into the world, the antichrist, the man of sin, cannot surface in the world until the Holy Spirit leaves the world. He (Holy Spirit) will be taken away out of the world at rapture with the believers in Christ. Hence, the rapture gives way to the devil to establish his kingdom on earth for seven years. Then shall be fulfilled the prophecy,

Woe to the inhabiters of the earth and of the sea! For the devil is come down unto you, having great wrath, because he knoweth that he hath but a short time. Revelation 12:12.

In contrast with the rapture, the second advent of Christ eliminates the kingdom of Satan and ushers in the establishment of the reign of Christ for one thousand years on earth.

At rapture, He will come as the Bridegroom to take unto Himself pure and holy brides. Eph 5:27; John 14:1-3 while at the second advent, he will come back with the brides to rule the nations and to set up His millennial kingdom on earth.

Behold, he cometh with clouds; and every eye shall see him, and they also which pierced him: and all kindreds of the earth shall wail because of him. Even so, Amen. Revelation 1:7.

"And Enoch also, the seventh from Adam, prophesied of these, saying, Behold, the Lord cometh with ten thousands of his saints, To execute judgment upon all, and to convince all that are ungodly among them of all their ungodly deeds which they have ungodly committed, and of all their hard speeches which ungodly sinners have spoken against him. Jude 14, 15.

At the rapture, He will come to meet believers in the cloud, 1 Thessalonians 4:17 while at the Second Advent, He will come to the earth in His majesty and His feet shall stand on mount Olives in Jerusalem.

"Then shall the LORD go forth, and fight against those nations, as when he fought in the day of battle. And his feet shall stand in that day upon the mount of Olives, which is before Jerusalem on the east, and the mount of Olives shall cleave in the midst thereof toward the east and toward the west, and there shall be a very great valley; and half of the mountain shall remove toward the north, and half of it toward the south. And ye shall flee to the valley of the mountains; for the valley of the mountains shall reach unto Azal: yea, ye shall flee, like as ye fled from before the earthquake in the days of Uzziah king of Judah: and the LORD my God shall come, and all the saints with thee. Zechariah 14:3, 5.

The rapture may occur at any moment 1 Cor 15:51-53, Phil 3:20-21 while the

Second Advent cannot occur until the antichrist has been revealed and the great tribulation transpires on earth. Matthew 24:29, 30, 2 Thess 2:3-10.

At rapture, only the believers in Christ will rise to meet the Lord in the air whereas at Second Advent, both Old Testament saints and those that were saved during the great tribulation together with the saints that have gone on rapture will reign with Christ for one thousand (1000) years.

The rapture is meant to keep the saints away from the rule of the antichrist on earth. 2 Tim 4:8, 1 Cor 13-15 while at Second Advent, the saints will rule with Christ on earth. Rev 2:26,27; 19:14

The saints will be taken for reward at the judgment seat of Christ (Bema) at rapture. **1 Corinthians 3:13-15.** The

Second Advent will put an end to the great tribulation thereby, it will be a comfort to great tribulation saints on earth especially Israel.

And so all Israel shall be saved: as it is written, There shall come out of Sion the Deliverer, and shall turn away ungodliness from Jacob: Romans 11:26.

ESCHATOLOGICAL EVENTS FROM THE TIME OF THE RAPTURE.

1. The rapture of the saints. 1 Thessalonians 4:16

2. The great tribulation on earth for seven years. Daniel 9:27

3. The marriage supper will take place in heaven simultaneously with the great tribulation. Revelation 19:7

4. The judgment seat of Christ (bema), also in heaven. 2 Corinthians 5:10

5. The second advent of Christ. Revelation 19:11-15

6. The battle of Armageddon. Revelation 16:13-16

7. Satan will be bound for 1000 years. Revelation 20:1, 2

8. The millennial reign of Christ. Revelation 20:4

9. Satan will be loose for a while to try the children that will be born in the millennial reign. Revelation 20:7, 8

10. The final battle of Gog and Magog. Revelation 20:8

11. The white throne judgment. Revelation 20:11

12. The lake of fire for the unrepentant sinners. Revelation 20:15

13. The new heaven and new earth for all the saints of God. Revelation 21:1

CHAPTER 3

THE DESCRIPTION OF THE RAPTURE

"Now this I say, brethren, that flesh and blood cannot inherit the kingdom of God; neither doth corruption inherit incorruption. Behold, I shew you a mystery; We shall not all sleep, but we shall all be changed, In a moment, in the twinkling of an eye, at the last trump: for the trumpet shall sound, and the dead shall be RAISED incorruptible, and we shall be changed, 1 Corinthians 15:50-52. ***But the day of the Lord will come as a thief in the night*** 2 Peter 3:10.

Obviously, thieves do not give notice of the day and the time they will come to rob people. If they do, no one will be foolish to sleep at such an hour. The people concerned will either prepare to fight them or escape for their lives. The coming of the Lord is likened to the sudden invasion of thieves in the night. At such times that the neighbours cannot come to rescue and the victims will be at the mercy of the robbers. Similarly, the Lord Jesus will come for the saints when they least expect. What do you think will happen if an angel blows a trumpet today telling the whole world that Jesus will come at a certain time tomorrow? Churches will be filled with emergency worshippers who will be begging God for the forgiveness of their sins.

In contrast, the Bible says,

Then shall two be in the field, the one shall be taken, and the other left. Two women shall be grinding at the mill; the one shall be taken, and the other left. Matthew 24:40,41.

You will be in the field of human endeavour when the trumpet will sound. That is, you will be going about your daily businesses and activities as usual. In fact, your normal ways of life will go on when Jesus will appear. Your normal life of anger, lying, fighting, grudges, rebellion, quarreling with your spouse. You can't pretend to be otherwise. Two people will be going to work, and they will be discussing from the abundance of things in their hearts, suddenly, the trumpet will sound. The righteous will be taken and the ungodly will be left behind. Some will be at work embezzling money when the coming of Christ will meet them unawares. Some will even be in the church serving the Lord they have not met when the trumpet will sound. Some will be on board in the plane and others in trains, vehicles, motorcycles and so on when it will sound. Where you are will determine what will be your fate on that day. This is because some people will die in the course of this great event and would not be found and when people search for them and do not find them, they may conclude that they have gone to meet the Lord whereas they have died and gone to hell. Where will you be when the first trumpet sounds?

The judgement day is drawing nigh Where shall I be?
When God the work of men shall try Where shall I be?
When east and west the fire will roll Where shall I be?

How will it be with my poor
soul Where shall I be?

Oh, where shall I be
When the first trumpet
sounds Oh, where shall I
be
When it sounds so loud
When it sound so loud as to wake up
the dead Oh, where shall I be when it
sounds

When wicked men his wrath
shall see Where shall I be?
And to the rocks and
mountains flee Where shall I
be?
When hills and
mountains flee Where
shall I be?
And all the work of men
decay Where shall I be?

When the saviour reigns from shore to
shore Where shall I be?

From Gods angry presence thrown Where shall I be?
Well, Ill be sleeping in my grave When the first trumpet sounds I'll be sleeping in my grave
When it sounds so loud
When it sounds so loud as to wake up the dead I'll be sleeping in my grave when it sounds

By The Carter Family

Thus you must know that this physical body cannot inherit the kingdom of God. Though we spend much for its comfort, it has no future! It ends in decay.

Now this I say, brethren, that flesh and blood cannot inherit the kingdom of God; neither doth corruption inherit incorruption. 1 Corinthians 15:50

God has taken flesh and blood to judgment. His verdict is that flesh and blood will not take part in the kingdom of God. Its lot and portion is decayed. Neither will it go to hell nor heaven. It is corrupt beyond repair. It is a pity that many Christians spend much of their money and time to adorn the flesh that has no future. As many that gratify the desire of the flesh cannot please God and would have no part in the kingdom of God. Hence, it is important to live your life to please God if you want to be raptured. The flesh and blood you spend the highest percentage of your income on has no future. The Lord Jesus warns,

And take heed to yourselves, lest at any time your hearts be overcharged with surfeiting, drunkenness, and cares of this life, and so that day come upon you unawares. For as a snare shall it come on all them that dwell on the face of the whole earth. Luke 21:34, 35.

And as it was in the days of Noe, so shall it be also in the days of the son of man. They did eat, they drank, they married wives, they were given in marriage, until the day that Noe entered in the ark, and the flood came, and destroyed them all. Likewise also as it was in the days of Lot; they did eat, they drank, they bought, they sold, they planted, they builded; But the same day that Lot went out of Sodom, it rained fire and brimstone from heaven, and destroyed all. Luke 17:26-29

Of every clean beast thou shall take to thee by sevens, the male and his female; and of beast that are not clean by two, the

male and his female for yet seven days ,and I will cause it to rain upon the earth forty days and forty night Genesis 7:2-4.

Seven days of grace were given to bring in all kinds of animals and birds. The impenitent sinners of the days of Noah would not utilize the last day of grace by turning to God in repentance. They saw animals going in but celebration, festivity and personal businesses would not allow them to go in.

Don't be overcharged with food, work, activities and the cares of this life. They will hinder many believers from going with this first flight. At this trumpet, all the true born again Christians will receive immortal bodies. This mortal body will be changed to an immortal (glorious and incorruptible body).

Behold, I shew you a mystery; we shall not all sleep, but we shall all be changed, in a moment, in a twinkling of an eye at the last trump; for the trump shall sound, and the dead shall be raised incorruptible, and we shall be changed. 1 Corinthians 15:51, 52.

At rapture, the dead in Christ will rise first though their bodies had been subjected and released to corruption (decay), they will be raised from the dead with incorruptible bodies; we which are alive will be caught up to meet the Lord in the air. 1 Thess 4:15, 17. At the sound of the last trump, we shall be changed from this corruptible body to a glorious body to meet the Lord in heaven. The time will be so sudden; in a moment, in the twinkling of an eye. In less than a second, the other person has vanished from sight. There will be no room for amendment once you are left behind. No second chance for careless

Christians. No second rapture. The only choice is to fight for your salvation with your own blood if you are privileged not to have died by accident. You have to face the wrath of God and of the antichrist in the great tribulation that will transpire on earth for seven years. I pray you will not fall victim to that horrible day of sorrow. (Amen)

CHAPTER 4

THE DEFINITE TIME OF THE RAPTURE

WHEN SHALL THESE THINGS BE?

The *disciples asked Jesus. The disciples were so eager to know the time because all that they valued was predicted for destruction by the Lord.*

And as he sat upon the mount of Olives, the disciples came unto him privately, saying, Tell us, when shall these things be? and what shall be the sign of thy coming, and of the end of the world,? Matthew 24:3.

The time of the rapture is not known to man.

"But of that day and hour knoweth no man, no, not the angels of heaven, but my Father only, Matthew 24:36. **Known unto God are all His works from the beginning of the world.** Acts15:18.

God does not do anything without attaching time. All his works are planned and programmed from the foundation of the world. He does nothing by chance. He determines all that will happen and directs the course of ALL His works.

Though we are not given the actual day and the exact hour Christ will come, we are given the signs of the end time. The fulfillment of these signs around us is evidence that the coming of Christ is imminent. It shows the wise saints that we are in the last days. Therefore, we must not be negligent about the time we are in. Jesus reproved the Pharisees of His days for their failure to study the time of His first coming.

And he said also to the people, when ye see a cloud rise out of the west, straight way ye say, there cometh a shower; and so it is. And when ye see the south wind blow, ye say, there will be heat; and it cometh to pass. Ye hypocrites, ye can discern the face of the sky and of the earth; but how is it that ye do not discern this time? Luke 12:54-56.

Since they did not bother to study the time, they knew not when the signs of his first coming were fulfilled. Consequently, when Jesus finally arrived and His star was glittering in the sky, they did not see it. Though the wise men who saw the star and followed its direction came to enquire from them, they did not believe.

Take heed, brethren, lest there be in any of you an evil heart of unbelief Hebrews 3:12. Jesus told the people of His days, ***The time is fulfilled, and the***

kingdom of God is at hand; repent ye and believe the gospel. Mark 1:15.

This explicitly reveals that there was a set time for the first coming that was fulfilled. Every plan and purpose of God under heaven has a time schedule.

To every thing there is a season and time to every purpose under heaven. Ecclesiastes 3:1.

Therefore, it is imperative to study the schedule of time for the first phase of the second advent of Christ. In the study of the end time event called ***Eschatology***, there is a time given to the Gentiles called the ***Time of Grace***. It is also referred to as the time of the Gentiles. This time began from the death and resurrection of our Lord and Saviour, Jesus Christ. You know that everything that has a beginning has an end. Your understanding of the time we are will help you to see the urgent need to prepare for the rapture. In view of this, we shall consider the predictions of when the time of the Gentiles (Time of Grace) will come to an end.

(a)**The Prediction of Jerusalems Independence from the Gentiles:** ***And they shall fall by the edge of the sword, and shall be led away captive into all nations: and Jerusalem shall be trodden down of the Gentiles, UNTIL THE TIME OF THE GENTILES BE FULFILLED,*** Luke 21:24. ***For I would not, brethren, that ye should be ignorant of this mystery, lest ye should be wise in your own conceits; that blindness in part is happened to Israel, until the fullness of the Gentiles be come in.*** Romans

11:25.

The above scriptures reveal that there is a time allotted to the Gentiles. This time of the Gentiles (Time of grace) will continue as long as Jerusalem remains under the control of the Gentiles. In other words, once Jerusalem is free from the control of the Gentiles, the fullness of the Gentiles has come.

This means the time of grace would come to its extreme end once Israel fully recovers Jerusalem from the Gentiles. In AD 70, the armies of General Titus invaded the city of Jerusalem, burned it with fire and the people scattered into captivity to all nations. Since then, the Jews had been longing for the sacred land. Their constant prayer was next year in Jerusalem. In the following centuries, the city was built at various times but suffered again and again under a similar fate- The Romans, Arabs and Turks in turn overran the city. It was a great day of joy for Israel when they gained their independence on 15th May, 1948.

Moreover, in 1967, seven (7) Arab nations were committed to driving the Jewish into the sea after their independence on May 15, 1948. Syria rose for a battle of annihilation of Zionist on 20 May, 1967, on May 27, Egypt challenged to stop the existence of Israel. May 30, 1967, the armies of Egypt, Jordan, Syrian, and Lebanon poised on the borders of Israel. The armies of Iraq, Algeria, Kuwait, Sudan and the whole Arab nations joined to eliminate Israel. Major General Ezer Weizmann an Israelite who is an eye witness, declared that the victory of the battle was brought by the finger of God. The Jews killed twenty-one thousand (21,000) of their enemies and lost 779 armies in the battle. And on June 7, 1967, the Jews took over the control of Jerusalem. John Hagee. Of course, that was a miracle.

However, the Palestinians lay claim on Haram al-sharif area of Jerusalem, the third holiest site in Islam. For many decades, there have been constant conflicts between the Israelis and the Palestinians on the issue of boundaries. Both the Palestines and Israelis claim Jerusalem as their capital, and the city contains sites sacred to both Jews and Muslims. Though Israel's parliament and Prime Minister's home are in Jerusalem, they sit in west Jerusalem, on the side of the city Israel has controlled since 1949. Israel captured East

Jerusalem in 1967 and annexed half of the city.

On 6th December, 2017, US president Donald Trump declared Jerusalem to be the capital of Israel. He also moved the embassy of the US in Israel from Tel AVIV to Jerusalem. Israel has taken over Jerusalem and the time of the Gentiles is to last till Israel will take over Jerusalem. Does this make it clear enough that the time of the Gentiles (the time of Grace) has been exhausted and the rapture can take place any moment from now? Are you ready for the glorious rapture of the saints in Christ?

(b). A day for a millennium Prediction: ***"But, beloved, be not ignorant of*** **this one thing, that one day is with the Lord as a thousand years,** ***and a thousand years as one day.*** 2 Peter 3:8, Psalms 90:4.

Since a thousand year with the Lord is one day and a day is also equivalent to a millennium, it is important we consider some Bible prophecies in the light of this equation; one day with man is equal to one thousand years with the Lord. 1d=1000y, where d stands for day and y for year respectively.

(I) **The comments of Jesus Christ:** ***And he said unto them, Go ye, and tell that fox, Behold, I cast out devils, and I do cures to day and to morrow, and the third day I shall be perfected. Nevertheless, I must work to day, and to morrow, and the day following: for it cannot be that a***

> ***prophet perish out of Jerusalem.***
> Luke 13:32-33.

Can this statement be referring to the death and resurrection of Christ? I don't think so, since His work did not end at His resurrection. A close look at the scripture verses shows His work cannot be made perfect until He has harvested His own saints on earth. He is still casting out the devils and He is still curing today. After His one thousand years of reigning on earth, called Millennium reign, he will not need to cast out devils or cure again since the saints would have been made perfect with Him. Even at the right hand of God, he continues to intercede for us till now.

"Who is he that condemneth? It is Christ that died, yea rather, that is risen again, who is even at the right hand of

God, who also maketh intercession for us. Romans 8:34

Hence, we shall apply a day for a thousand years, ***Behold, I cast out devils and I do cures today and tomorrow, and the third day I shall be perfected.*** This could be referring to the two thousand years given for the time of grace in which Christ would work and would gather His saints on the third day of His perfection in a thousand years of millennial reign of Christ.

(II) The Prophecy of Hosea. ***After two days will he revive us: in the third day he will raise us up, and we shall live in his sight.*** Hosea 6:2.

In the same vein, After two days shows that he has two days to work, which is equivalent to two thousand years (2,000 years). We have used the time, the rapture is what we are waiting for so that His work can be made perfect on the third day that is standing for the millennial reign. With this prophecy, the Israelites hope to be revived after two days at the great tribulation and subsequently be raised up to reign with Christ on the third day, which is the one thousand years of Christ reign on earth.

(III) The six Days of Creation and the seventh day of Rest: God used six days to work in the creation of the universe and He rested on the seventh day. Some Bible scholars proved that God has six days to work and it is equivalent to six thousand years. The 7th day is the one thousand years for the millennial reign of Christ. It is proved that from the time of creation to the time God destroyed the living creatures on earth with flood were two days- which is two thousand years. And from the flood to the time of resurrection of Christ were another two days (standing for another two thousand years). From the ascension of Christ till year two thousand was another two days that were supposed to be the last days of work. If we draw a conclusion from this, we can see that the time of the Gentiles (Time of Grace) has elapsed in the year 2000.

Hence, Jesus ought to have come before or at the year 2000. I strongly believed these theories, and was earnestly anticipating the rapture. In 1998, I preached on the subject of rapture on one particular Sunday. As I was sleeping, around 1am, I suddenly heard a very loud sound that woke me from sleep and it sounded like a trumpet in my ears. I raised my two hands on my bed and shouted, Blessed is He that cometh in the name of the Lord. While I waited for a couple of minutes to be caught up (raptured), I heard the second sound again; it was a big lorry that was honking! This is to tell you the extent to which I was prepared. Are you prepared? Do you have this hope in you?

And every man that has this hope in him purifieth himself even as he is pure. 1 John 3:3.

Can you say you are pure? You must make your way right with God now as you bow to talk to God. Stop wasting your life on the ephemeral pleasure of this world.

"And that, knowing the time, that now it is high time to awake out of sleep: for now is our salvation nearer than when we believed. The night is far spent, the

day is at hand: let us therefore cast off the works of darkness, and let us put on the armour of light. Let us walk honestly, as in the day; not in rioting and drunkenness, not in chambering and wantonness, not in strife and envying. But put ye on the Lord Jesus Christ, and make not provision for the flesh, to fulfil the lusts thereof. Romans 13:11-14.

Oh let's not be ignorant of this time of peril. Let us rise as children of light and wake our wearied and slumbering brethren. You can now see the wall clock of end time events that our time is far spent. The night is almost gone. The dawn of the resurrection morning will soon break in.

Questions: Why did Jesus not come before or at the year 2000?

What can we call this time we are?

These and many others will be discussed in the next chapter.

CHAPTER 5

THE DELAY OF HIS COMING AND THE DEPARTURE FROM THE TRUTH

While the bridegroom tarried, they all slumbered and slept. Matthew 25:5.

In the previous chapter, we saw the Biblical and theological theories showing that the time given to the Gentiles has elapsed. In the year 2000 AD, I was eagerly expecting the Lord Jesus to come for

His elect. I saw the year as the last year the Gentiles had in the theory of time. Hence, I wholly set myself apart from God and lived as if the rapture would take place in the next moment. While I waited till the last day of the year, I was still earnestly expectant till the shout of happy New Year, 2001.

I was so disturbed because I felt the

theories had actually failed. While I wondered why it should be so, I discovered in my sequence study of the bible about the end time, that the bridegroom will actually delay. ***While the bridegroom tarries*** This statement shows that there is a set time in God's programme, the bridegroom needs to come but would be delayed in His coming.

No one is said to be late when there is no stipulated time for the assignment given to him to do. Likewise, you cannot claim that a person is late for a programme when there is no set time for arrival. The parable of the ten virgins is referring to those who are saved by the atoning blood of the Lamb. People that are saved during the time of the Gentiles (Time of Grace) are Brides of Christ and Jesus Christ is the

Bridegroom.

He that hath the bride is the bridegroom: but the friend of the bridegroom, which standeth and heareth him, rejoiceth greatly because of the bridegrooms voice: this my joy therefore is fulfilled. John 3:29. For I am jealous over you with godly jealousy: for I have espoused you to one husband, that I may present you as a chaste virgin to Christ. 2 Corinthians 11:2

Everyone that is able to go with Him at rapture shall partake in the marriage supper of the lamb. Therefore, Jesus Christ, the Bridegroom would not come in the year 2000 because it is already in God's programme that He will delay in His coming. The time we are is the time He tarries or delays. It is sure He would not spend another millennium before He returns.

"The Lord is not slack concerning his promise, as some men count slackness; but is longsuffering to us-ward, not willing that any should perish, but that all should come to repentance. *2* Peter 3:9.

What are you doing as a Christian to rescue the unsaved souls from the danger of God's wrath that is looming upon the world? Can you pretend not to know that the time is short? You cannot be silent and be guiltless. Rise up with this mid-night cry and wake the slumbering and sleeping souls. The time of the Gentiles has expired. The time we are is the time of His patience. He is not willing that any should perish but that all might repent of their secret sins and be saved through His finished work of redemption on the cross. Why are you wasting this extra time given to you in His abundant mercy? The whistle may blow at any time and the injury time will be over. If you spurn this precious warning, where will you hide your shameful face when you are left behind.

Careless soul why
will you linger
Wand ring from
the fold of God?
Hear you not the
invitation?
Oh prepared to meet thy God

Careless soul, oh
heed the warning
For your life will
soon be gone
Oh how sad to face the
judgement
Unprepared to meet
thy God

Why so thoughtless
are you standing?
While the fleeting

years go by,
And your life is
spent in folly?
Oh prepared to
meet thy God.

Hear you not the
earnest pleadings
Of your friends that
wish you well?
And perhaps before
tomorrow
You'll be called to
meet thy God

If you spurn
the invitation
Till thy spirit
shall depart
Then you'll see you're
sad condition
Unprepared to meet
thy God

By James H.

Stanley, 1909

Looking at the last day of Lot and his family in Sodom before the angel poured the wrath of his indignation without mixture on Sodom and Gomorrah, the angels hastened Lot to take his wife and his two daughters out of Sodom.

And when the morning arose, then the angels hastened Lot, saying, arise, take thy wife, and thy two daughters, which are here; lest thou be consumed in the iniquity of the city. And while he lingered, the men laid hold upon his hand and upon the hand of his wife, and upon the hand of his two daughters; the Lord being merciful unto him: and they brought him forth, and set him without the city. Genesis 19:15, 16.

It was a fearful warning that they would be consumed in the iniquity of the city if they refused to leave. Despite the instruction was urgent, Lot lingered. Hastened, yet he delayed. Similarly, there are many people God has warned severally to leave their sodomic lifestyles but they remain sluggish in the world system. Lot was saddled with the responsibility of taking his wife and his two children out. It is incumbent on every parent to bring their spouse and children out of Sodom. You cannot be held guiltless as a Christian parent while you fold your hands and watch your children in worldly and devilish attires. Your silence means consent. You will be held responsible. You claim to be born again but the ephemerals of this world bog you down in this present day Sodom.

Love not the world, neither the things that are in the world. If any man love the world, the love of the Father is not in him." 1 John 2:15.

Ye adulterers and adulteresses, know ye not that the friendship of the world is enmity with God? Whosoever therefore will be a friend of the world is the enemy

of God. James 4:4.

What are the things God has been warning you over and over again to leave or forsake and you remain adamant? What is it that holds you to the world system when judgment is looming over the world? If you are not ready to leave the world system, be prepared to perish with the world as Lot was told. The situation may be beyond your human effort, as it was with Lot, the power of God will break all the tyranny of Satan over your life in Jesus name, amen. While Lot himself would not leave Sodom, let alone, helping his family to leave, the Lord being merciful to him, caused the angels to hold his hand, the hand of his wife, and of his two daughters and dragged them out. The hand of God's mercy is widely opened to help you out of Sodom if you are willing to come and place your hands in His hand.

Why will you linger when the hands of

His mercy are opened, waiting for a penitent child to receive. Why will you wait to mourn and wail for mercy when God has slammed the gate of mercy against you? Come now to Jesus. Don't waste this precious time extended for the sake of your salvation. Your time is over but you can still escape through this extension of His mercy. Come to Him now, He will in no wise cast you out.

They all slumbered and slept.

At the delay of the bridegroom, the brides relaxed. The urgency of the time at which they expected Him prompted them to prepare and make themselves ready. Initially, they were eager to see Him and were not tired of pressing forward to see Him. However, when He tarried, discouragement set in and they thought to wait a moment to rest but began to slumber and subsequently slept. A little rest can lead to a deep sleep. Watch out: Are you not sleeping? Where are the fathers of faith in this generation, who witnessed the revival of the 70s and early 80s? What are you doing to maintain the fire of the faith that was handed over to us? About three decades ago when I met the Lord, the messages of rapture and the second coming were so rampant.

The fire within and the urgency of the rapture propelled us to seek the lost. Today, rapture is becoming strange on the pulpit. Some of the preachers who care to mention it, did it in a trivialised manner. Since the year 2000, many churches have declined in the standard of holiness as if Christ will not come again. Many relax in evangelism, rest in prayer for the lost souls and slumber in unrighteous gain at the expense of unrighteous souls. This is seriously terrifying! The church for which Jesus died is deeply sleeping in sin.

The beauty and glory of the church has been holiness, which many preachers have slain on the altar of seeking fame, finance and women. It is disheartening that such sins that should not be heard among the ungodly are being perpetrated in the churches of the living God. Many faithful ministers of God have departed from the truth. Many godly Christians have deviated from the faith that was once delivered to the saints. Many habits, manners and dresses we know to be worldly and devilish are paraded as fashion. Ladies dress to church half naked, without a sense of shame. The church that is supposed to be a ground of liberation from sin becomes a place of liberty for sin. Many churches become a ground to show fashion instead of the given responsibility to show people their iniquities and sins. Isaiah 58:1, 2, Peter 3:3- 5; 9, 10. People seek for a haven of rest instead of heaven. Many ministers are devoted to competition instead of consecration; they care more for happiness of people than for their holiness; care for applause of men than for God's approval; search for green pasture rather than seeking for God's power. We have men of charisma without character. Men who emphasize more on prosperity than on purity. Likewise, the people turn their ears away from the truth into fables.

"For the time will come when they will not endure sound doctrine; but after their own lusts shall they heap to themselves teachers, having itching ears; And they shall turn away their ears from the truth, and shall be turned unto fables. 2 Timothy 4:3, 4.

Such are sycophants and praise-singers who applaud motivational preachers that entertain them with jokes and comedy on the altar. Brutish preachers with a loose and flamboyant life are gone out to deceive gullible souls.

But they shall proceed no further; for their folly shall be manifest unto all men, 2 Timothy 3:9.

The rapture will actually expose these unscrupulous and fake preachers, and the pretentious Christians but it will be too late for those that are deceived. You better escape for your life.

"And with all deceivableness of unrighteousness in them that perish; because they received not the love of the truth, that they might be saved. And for this cause God shall send them strong delusion, that they should believe a lie: That they all might be damned who believed not the truth, but had pleasure in unrighteousness. 2 Thessalonians 2:10-12.

CHAPTER 6

THE DECLARATION OF THE RAPTURE

Notices of war were made by the blowing of trumpets in the days of old. And nobody prepares for battle if the trumpet does not make a clear sound. 1 Corinthians 14:8.

The notice of the rapture in the scripture is clear and beyond doubt. Whoever pretends not to know deliberately refuses to prepare for the rapture. God does not want us to be unaware so He spread the notice of Christ's second coming across the scripture, it is spread across the old and new Testaments.

More so, God has raised some of His servants to alert His children of the imminent appearance of Christ in the air.

And the gospel of the kingdom shall be preached in all the world for a witness unto them. Matthew 24:14.

The gospel of the second coming of Christ will only serve as a witness to many people that heard it but rejected it. The refusal of men cannot stop the fulfillment of God's word.

Apostle Paul explicitly assured the believers in Christ of the hope we have on those who slept in the Lord. This should serve as a comfort to us and our brethren who died in Christ.

"But I would not have you to be ignorant, brethren, concerning them which are asleep, that ye sorrow not, even as others which have no hope. For if we believe that Jesus died and rose again, even so them also which sleep in Jesus will God bring with him. For this we say unto you by the word of the Lord, that we which

are alive and remain unto the coming of the Lord shall not prevent them which are asleep. For the Lord himself shall descend from heaven with a shout, with the voice of the archangel, and with the trump of God: and the dead in Christ shall rise first: Then we which are alive and remain shall be caught up together with them in the clouds, to meet the Lord in the air: and so shall we ever be with the Lord. Wherefore comfort one another with these words.

1 Thessalonians 4:13-18.

Enoch also proclaimed the second advent of Christ.

And Enoch also, the seventh from Adam, prophesied of these, saying, Behold, the Lord cometh with ten thousands of his saints, To execute judgment upon all, and to convince all that are ungodly among them of all their ungodly deeds which they have ungodly committed, and of all their hard speeches which ungodly sinners have spoken against him. Jude 1:14-15.

By faith, Enoch, the seventh from Adam prophesied of the second advent of Christ. There was no Bible at that time yet he declared it accurately that the Lord will come and execute judgment upon the ungodly.

Our Lord Jesus Christ also emphasised His second advent.

And then shall appear the sign of the Son of man in heaven: and then shall all the tribes of the earth mourn, and they shall see the Son of man coming in the clouds of heaven with power and great glory. Matthew 24:30.

Jesus Christ laid emphasis in many parts of the scriptures about His second advent to avoid any element of doubt.

The angels also heralded His coming to assure all disciples and all that will be saved.

And while they looked stedfastly toward heaven as he went up, behold, two men stood by them in white apparel; Which also said, Ye men of Galilee, why stand ye gazing up into heaven? this same Jesus, which is taken up from you into heaven, SHALL SO COME IN LIKE MANNER AS YE HAVE SEEN HIM GO INTO HEAVEN. Acts 1:10-11.

This same Jesus that was despised and rejected by men, will come back for His saints in the same way.

Apostle Peter also stressed it.

"But the day of the Lord will come as a thief in the night; in which the heavens shall pass away with a great noise, and the elements shall melt with fervent heat, the earth also and the works that are therein shall be burned up. 2 Peter 3:10.

Moreover, God reveals the rapture of the saints to men of our contemporary to convince them of the need for them to prepare. At the translation of Elijah, God revealed to the sons of the prophet that they were in the cities they passed through when Elijah was to be taken away. And also to Elijah himself, he was aware before others that he would be taken away to heaven by whirlwind. The matter was also known to Elisha his disciple. 2 Kings 2:1-6. Likewise, there are many visions of the rapture by the genuine ministers of God calling us to prepare for the glorious day. From 1991 till date, I have had many visions of the imminent rapture of the saints. And my daughter has also testified to many visions the Lord revealed to her. This is the midnight cry calling all the brides of Christ to awake from sleep.

While the bridegroom tarried, they all slumbered and slept. And at midnight there was a cry made, Behold, the bridegroom cometh; go ye out to meet him. Then all those virgins arose, and trimmed their lamps. Matthew 25:5-7.

There have been incessant cries to awake the sleeping souls. God has been warning you through His word that the night is far spent and the need for you to cast off the work of darkness and be ready for the arrival of the Bridegroom. There are several revelations of the rapture and the signs of the end time coming to pass in our very eyes. Notwithstanding, many are still dull with hearing. People that will not heed the midnight cry will not hear the sound of the trumpet. To be forewarned is to be forearmed. The trumpet has made a clear sound. Only the cowards will not prepare for battle. If you claim not to know, then you willingly choose to be ignorant.

For this they willingly are ignorant. 2 Peter 3:5.

CHAPTER 7

THE DELIBERATE DECISION OF THE WISE SAINTS

"Then shall the kingdom of heaven be likened unto ten virgins, which took their lamps, and went forth to meet the bridegroom. And five of them were wise, and five were foolish. They that were foolish took their lamps, and took no oil with them: But the wise took oil in their vessels with their lamps. While the bridegroom tarried, they all slumbered and slept. And at midnight there was a cry made, Behold, the bridegroom cometh; go ye out to meet him. Then all those virgins arose, and trimmed their lamps. And the foolish said unto the wise, Give us of your oil; for our lamps are gone out. But the wise answered, saying, Not so; lest there be not enough for us and you: but go ye rather to them that sell, and buy for yourselves. And while they went to buy, the bridegroom came;

and they that were ready went in with him to the marriage: and the door was shut, *Matthew 25:1-10. 1 John 3:1-3, 2 Cor 5:1-4 (LB), Hebrews 12:12.*

Jesus Christ likened the preparation of the saints to the parable of the ten virgins, who took their lamps and they all went to meet the bridegroom.
They were all virgins – which means they had been washed from their sins. They had been saved and sanctified. They all took their lamps which implies that they took the word of God serious and they allowed God's word to direct, guide and shed light to their paths. Psalm 119:105. Their faith and hope in their journey to see the bridegroom were sustained by the word of God (the lamp).

The oil is the one that fuels the lamp to lighten the road. This is the measure of inner grace, insight into the revelation of God's word or anointing, that is generated by the Holy Spirit when we are in place of prayer. It causes the word of God to burn like fire in us to obey God. It is the supernatural working of grace by the Holy Spirit to accomplish what human nature cannot do.

Let us therefore come boldly unto the throne of grace, that we may obtain mercy, and find grace to help in time of need, Hebrews 4:16. But ye, beloved, building up yourselves on your most holy faith, praying in the Holy Ghost. Jude v20.

Hence, the wise virgins secured it freely on their knees in prayer. They deliberately secured extra oil since they didn't know how long the journey would take them. When the bridegroom would not come at the time they supposed, they were worn out and they slept. However, the lamps were still consuming oil even when sleep would not allow them to generate more oil. The wise virgins had a foresight into the future and were ready to pay the price it might cost them to see the Bridegroom. They had secured grace to go the extra mile with God; thereby making themselves ready for the Bridegroom. When He came, they went in with Him into the marriage and the door was shut.

However, the foolish did not see the need to take extra oil in their bottles. When there was a cry in the mid-night, their lamps were already going out. The foolishness of the five foolish virgins was due to their nonchalant attitude to eternal matters. They lacked foresight and were only mindful of that present moment. They could respond to the word of God but would not find time to pray for grace. Their zeal did not go far. Being myopic in thinking, they didn't see the need for extra oil.

They did not consider that the Bridegroom could delay. They were complacent with the simplicity that is in Christ. They could not go the extra mile with God. They turned away from any service to Christ that seemed to be risky or stressful. Then, they needed oil urgently. Though they would not mind paying for what they refused to take freely, yet it was too late for them. The door of grace was already shut. They were told to go to those who sell. People who make merchandise of the gospel are the ones left for them to contact. Why will you delay till you will have to pay with your life, when the door of His grace is already slammed? If you will not utilise the free grace of salvation that is in Christ, be ready to pay for your salvation at the great tribulation.

How shall we escape, if we neglect so great salvation; which at the first began to be spoken by the Lord and was confirmed unto us by them that heard him. Hebrews 2:3.

Brethren, the fact of the rapture is certain and hence every wise believer must prepare both in HOLINESS and general Christian living and conduct. Everyone having this hope purifies himself even as Christ is pure. We must be diligent to be found of Him in peace without spot and blameless. 2 Peter 3:10-14, Hebrews 11:13-16.

CHAPTER 8

THE DESCENDING CHRIST AND THE DEPARTURE OF THE PURIFIED SAINTS

For the Lord Himself shall descend from heaven with a shout, with the voice of the archangel, and with the trump of God; and the dead in Christ shall rise first: Then we which are alive and remain shall be caught up together with them in the clouds, to meet the Lord in the air: and so shall we ever be with the Lord. 1 Thessalonians 4:16,17.

The Lord Himself

The Lord that would not be deceived by the title the church accorded you. The Lord Himself sees all workers of iniquities in the church; who declared to the church of Ephesus to go back to their first love, and was not deceived by all their commitment and faithfulness. The Lord Himself who knows that the church of Pergamos had embraced the doctrine of Balaam and discovered that the church of Thyatira had welcomed Jezebel the worldly woman into the church. The Lord Himself who knows all the gimmicks of the church of Sardis to keep their names popular and vibrant but did not notice that they were spiritually dead. The church of Laodicean boasted that they were rich but He fetched them out of their emptiness and showed them their abject poverty. What a costly assumption!

The Lord Himself sees unforgiveness in your heart though you said you have forgiven her. He who sees an indirect malice between you and your spouse. He who sees your backbiting is the One we are talking about. The Lord Himself who sees all the secret smoking and how you conceal your secret alcoholism with tom-tom and still function at the altar of God. The Lord Himself that is a living witness of your fornication and adultery which you cover up with prophecy and singing in the singing team. He who knows you are a liar and there is no truth in you though people are afraid to call you a liar (your real name) because of your ministerial appellation. It will be known on that day. The Lord Himself that sees all your unfaithfulness in the house of God and yet nobody dares to challenge you. He who sees when you change hundreds to thousands and commit fraud with government money. The Lord Himself sees all the church money you borrow and does not return it as a treasurer. What about the money you borrow and you quarrel with the owner whenever he/she asks for it? Pastor, what about the money you mismanage and you put it under miscellaneous expenses? The great Auditor General is coming to re-audit the account of His church. One who sees your refusal to restitute your way with all the warning of God. The Lord Himself that sees your immoral life of lesbianism, homosexuality and masturbation. The Lord that hears your immoral language and has been witness to your marital unfaithfulness with the wife of your youth.

"But I say unto you, That every idle word that men shall speak, they shall give account thereof in the day of judgment. Matthew 12:36.

The Lord that sees how you date three people at a time and you call yourself a brother or a sister. The Lord who knows your true identity that you are a brutal viper and not a brother, and a sinner and not a sister is the One coming for the saints. The Lord that sees you at your pornographic pictures and blue films on internet will apprehend you on that day though you seem to be zealous for God. The Lord whose eyes run to and fro throughout the whole earth and could see all the condom and contraceptive drugs in your bag as spinster and bachelor is the One coming. Before I got married, I did not know about condoms.

If I had seen it, I would have taken it for a balloon! The Lord that sees your secret abortions while you lied to the sympathizing brethren that you were sick. The Lord who knows how you hate and speak evil of Pastors He sent to tell you the truth. The Lord that knows what you call modern Christianity as meddling with the world and your so called fashion as fallacy and a fall from the truth. The Lord that knows you as Jezebel on the altar who dresses to corrupt, kill and deceive gullible souls. The Lord who knows you are a chameleon and a professional pretender, and that there is no way you can be caught in your ungodliness, is coming to fetch you out if you refuse to repent today.

Neither is there any creature that is not manifest in His sight: but all things are naked and opened unto the eye of Him with whom we have to do. Hebrews 4:13

Shall descend from heaven with a shout

The Lord is coming with a shout of victory, victory at last for the children of God. It will be a shout of unspeakable joy for all the tried and triumphant saints. The felicity of the believers who overcome sin, self and Satan will know no bounds. Beloved, what a day of joy that will be for the saints.

Therefore, the redeemed of the Lord shall return and everlasting joy shall be upon their head: they shall obtain gladness and joy; and sorrow and mourning shall flee away. Isaiah 51:11. ***Beloved, now are we the sons of God, and it doth not yet appear what we shall be: but we know that, when he shall appear, we shall be like him; for we shall see him as he is.*** 1 John 3:2.

It shall be a shout of everlasting separation from the ungodly.

Then shall two be in the field; the one shall be taken and the other left. Two women shall be grinding at the mill; the one shall be taken and the other left. Matthew 24:40, 41.

Will you be among the ones that will be taken or in the number of those that will be left? Don't be quick to answer. Check your life. Of course, it is a shout of distinction to put a clear difference between those who serve God and those that serve Him not.

"Then shall ye return, and discern between the righteous and the wicked, between him that serveth God and him that serveth him not. Malachi 3:18.

Those who serve God in holiness will be distinguished on that day. Since they have His nature, they will recognise His voice at His coming. Only those who hear will go on rapture at His coming.

Verily, verily I say unto you, the hour is coming and now is when the dead shall hear the voice of the Son of God and they that hear shall live. John 5:25.

The true believers in Christ will distinguish His voice from the noise in the world because they are familiar with it. A young man went to the river to take his bath. He decided to relax on a tree for some minutes before going back home, while he was on a tree, a shepherd came to the river with his flock to drink water. After a few minutes, another shepherd brought his flock of sheep to the same river to drink water. The man on the tree was thinking there would be a quarrel between the two shepherds on how to distinguish their sheep. Amazingly, when the first shepherd noticed that his sheep should have been satisfied with water, he shouted mene mene and all his sheep left the river and followed him!

And when he putteth forth his own sheep, he goeth before them and the sheep follow him for they KNOW HIS VOICE. John 10:4.

If you have not followed Him you cannot know his voice. If you don't know His voice now, you can't know it at rapture.

And with the trump of God.

In the days of old, notices of war were made by the blowing of the trumpet. The trumpet of God differs from that of men. The trumpets of men prepare men for war and bring trouble to men. However, the trumpet of God calls men out of trouble and gives them peace. It does not give space for men to prepare. It calls those who are prepared to rest and peace.

In a moment, in the twinkling of an eye, at the last trump: for the trumpet shall sound, and the dead shall be raised incorruptible, and we shall be changed, 1 Corinthians 15:52.

Hence, the trumpet of God is not meant to prepare men for the rapture but to bring prepared saints to their Lord and Saviour. Are you prepared?

and the dead in Christ shall rise first

The dead in Christ could not be referring to Old Testament saints who will resurrect at the second advent of Christ on earth after the great tribulation. Therefore, it refers to Christians who died under the atonement of the blood of Jesus Christ and the sacrifice of His body for sin once and for all.

For by one offering he hath perfected for ever them that are sanctified. Hebrew 10:14.

Obviously, anyone that has not received Jesus as Lord and personal Saviour cannot go with Him at rapture. This is because the rapture is meant only for those who are either alive in Christ or dead in Christ- awaiting resurrection. You can be in the church and not be in Christ. Being a member of a church does not mean you are in Christ. In the church, we have members that live in sin of fornication, adultery, drunkenness, fighting, stealing, lying etc and are choristers, ushers, deacons, evangelists, pastors, bishops, apostles, and so on. However, anyone who is in Christ does not continue in sin because there is no sin in Christ.

And ye know that he was manifested to take away sins; and in him is no sin. Whosoever abideth in him sinneth not: whosoever sinneth hath not seen him, neither known him. He that committeth sin is of the devil; for the devil sinneth from the beginning. For this purpose the son of God was manifested, that he might destroy the works of the devil. Whosoever is born of God doth not commit sin: for his seed remaineth in him; and he cannot sin, because he is born of God. 1 John 3:5, 6, 8, 9

There is no sin in Christ. Nobody should claim that he is in Christ while he lives in sin. Are you free from sin?

Then we which are alive

We who are alive and not yet dead in sin and trespasses like the brethren in the church of Sardis, who sustained a living name but are spiritually dead.

And unto the church of Sardis write I know thy works that thou hast a name that thou livest and art dead. Revelation 3:1.

Today, ministers of God add title to title to keep their name vibrant and relevant among Christians that are ignorant of their inner decay. Only those who are not dead in clamoring for title and making name for themselves are the living Christians Jesus is coming for. Those who lean not on name (title) but a pure Christian life as a proof of their worth in Christ.

We who are alive and are not just buried in church activities but are spiritually dead. We who are alive and are not dead in worldliness and worldly conduct.

Then, we which are alive in reading and meditating in his word to do according to what is written there; and in prayer and fasting in the closet seeking the face of God and His kingdom, then we which are alive in the great commission to warn the sinners of the great impending judgment that dangles precariously over the unsaved souls; and are in daily expectation of the rapture.

and not to me only, but unto all them also that love his appearing. 2 Timothy 4:8.

Are you still alive or you are dead? It is not too late for you to come to the Lord for mercy.

and *remain*

Then we who are alive and remain holy and uncorrupted in the midst of corruption and pollution in the world.

The believers that remain steadfast in their faith and are faithful and loyal to the Lord. Those who remain true and uncompromising in this corrupt and untoward generation; and also remain committed to the service of Christ and His work. Then we who are alive and remain soldiers of the cross, contending for the old time faith that was once delivered unto the saints shall be caught up together with them in the clouds, to meet the Lord in the sky. Beloved, can you imagine the thrill of indescribable joy at our meeting with the crucified Saviour. What a great day of joy it will be for me when I will meet my Saviour, Justifier, Sanctifier, Redeemer, Friend, my God and my long awaited King.

And so shall we ever be with the Lord.

We shall be with the Lord in the

splendour of His glory and honour to part no more – where there is no fear, hunger, pain, sickness, tears or sorrow again.

And God shall wipe away all tears from their eyes, and there shall be no more death, neither sorrow nor crying, neither shall there be any more pain: for the former things are passed away. And he that sat upon the throne said, behold, I make all things new. Revelation 21:4, 5. Will you be there?

CHAPTER 9

THE DISTRESS AND THE DOOM OF THE SKEPTICS

A natural man is skeptical of the things of the spirit. He hardly believes anything except the things that his eyes see. As we have skeptics today, even so were there many in the days of old. Still, their skepticism did not prevent the execution of God's plan and purpose. Your unbelief cannot stop the fulfillment of God's plan for His saints. The dwellers of Sodom and Gomorrah and the men and women of Noah's days, were all skeptical of God's impending judgements.

And Lot went out, and spake unto his sons in law, which married his daughters, and said, Up, get you out of this place; for the LORD will destroy this city, BUT HE SEEMED AS ONE THAT MOCKED UNTO HIS SONS IN LAW. Genesis 19:14

While they remained in disbelief and were still thinking of the emergency departure of Lot from Sodom, leaving his house and properties behind, the Lord rained brimstone and fired upon them.

Then the LORD rained upon Sodom and upon Gomorrah brimstone and fire from the LORD out of heaven; And he looked towards Sodom and Gomorrah, and toward all the land of the plain, and beheld, and, lo, the smoke of the country went up as the smoke of a furnace. Genesis 19:24, 28

They would have striven to escape but it was too late. They would have wished they believed Lot but they were already damned.

And they that went in, went in male and female of all flesh, as God had commanded Him: and the LORD shut him in. And the waters prevailed exceedingly upon the earth; and all high hills, that were under the whole heaven, were covered. Genesis 7:16; 19.

It is amazing that the animals heard the

inward call of God to go to Noah for salvation and they heeded the call to escape from the impending judgment of God.

"Yea, the stork in the heaven knoweth her appointed times; and the turtle and the crane and the swallow observe the time of their coming; but my people know not the judgment of the LORD. Jeremiah 8:7.

The people saw the domestic animals and the wild animals coming two by two into the ark yet they did not believe it. That alone was supposed to make them believe. However, when distress and anguish came upon them, they knew it was true but it was too late. The people believed when they became victims of the judgment but it was too late. If you fail to believe today, you will soon believe when you are left behind and will have to face the terrible torture of the antichrist and the wrath of God.

"Then shall two be in the field; the one shall be taken, and the other left. Two women shall be grinding at the mill; the one shall be taken, and the other left. Matthew 24:40, 41.

The rate of mortality will be so high at the time of the rapture, when the pilots disappear and the drivers of some vehicles also would have gone, those on board will perish and there will be commotion and lots of accidents on the roads. Many people will die and many maimed in the process of the rapture. Whoever dies in the course of the rapture will end up in hell fire. Many people that would be declared missing may not have gone on rapture but are dead and are given mass burial in order to avoid environmental pollution.

Hospitals will be filled with accident victims and many of them will have to be rejected.

I was at Federal Medical Centre Lokoja in 2017 and some accident victims were brought to the hospital, but the accident and emergency ward was already filled to the door and even passages. The Hospital Management could not help in this situation. The victims were dropped outside where they groaned in pain while bleeding on the floor and were dying one after the other. The sympathisers were shouting but could not help. The day of rapture will be more terrible than that because it is a world-wide event and there will be accidents in every place. Many accident victims will shout for help but none will be there to help them.

They will die in regrets and pains. The law enforcement agency will not be able to help the situation as they see a mammoth crowd coming to report the missing of their children and their loved ones. People will be greatly distressed and in despair of life and in total depression. Many careless Christians that would be left behind will cry and weep bitterly for a second chance but none will hear their desperate and importunate prayers for the second rapture. They will openly confess all their secret sins in tears but their repentance would be too late.

Because I have called, and ye refused; I have stretched out my hand, and no man regarded; But ye have set at nought all my counsel, and would none of my reproof: I also will laugh at your calamity; I will mock when your fear cometh; When your fear cometh as desolation, and your destruction cometh as a whirlwind; when distress and anguish cometh upon you. Then shall they call upon me, but I will not answer; they shall seek me early, but they shall not find me: Proverbs 1:24-28

Like the rich man offered a fervent and passionate prayer for mercy when the door of mercy was already closed. He had to face the consequence of his carelessness in the torment of the fiery flame of unquenchable fire in hell.

There was a certain rich man, which was clothed in purple and fine linen, and fared

sumptuously every day: And there was a certain beggar named Lazarus, which was laid at his gate, full of sores, And desiring to be fed with the crumbs which fell from the rich mans table: moreover the dogs came and licked his sores. And it came to pass, that the beggar died, and was carried by the angels into Abrahams bosom: the rich man also died, and was buried; And in hell he lift up his eyes, being in torments, and seeth Abraham afar off, and Lazarus in his bosom. And he cried and said, Father Abraham, have mercy on me, and send Lazarus, that he may dip the tip of his finger in water, and cool my tongue; for I am tormented in this flame. But Abraham said, Son, remember that thou in thy lifetime receivedst thy good things, and likewise Lazarus evil things: but now he is comforted, and thou art tormented. Luke 16:19-25.

When the rich man opened his eyes, the record of his wealth was not found. He found himself being tormented by the horrible flame of hell. He stood his ground to offer a fervent but unanswered prayer. His first response to the torment of hell was to pray for mercy. If he had cared to pray on earth, that might have been against his enemies. He had no time to pray for repentance, but at last, he had time to die. He prayed for mercy and asked for a drop of water but he never knew that an iota of mercy cannot be found after death. None of his requests were answered. Look at the response of Abraham to his passionate prayer: ***"But Abraham said, son, remember..."***

You will be called to remember how you have spent your life without retaining God in your knowledge. Remember the opportunity God gave you to repent but you blew it off. Remember how you looked down and despised the people God sent to show you the way of life. Remember how God called you to obtain mercy again and again through the death of Christ Jesus but you did not take His counsel.

In the same way, all that would be left behind at rapture will have to face the consequence of their carelessness as they would face an unspeakable torture of the antichrist in seven years of great tribulation on earth.

If they want to be saved, they will have to pay for their salvation with their own blood for despising the gracious offer of free pardon for salvation. Those that will be left after the believers must have gone on rapture will remember that they were told to prepare. They will weep and none will wipe away their tears. The fear of torture and of terror will kill them before they are confronted with it.

"Mens hearts failing them for fear, and for looking after those things which are coming on the earth: for the powers of heaven shall be shaken. Luke 21:26.

Their regret will be great and their weeping and sorrow will be without comfort. Why will you wait till the day of mercy has passed you by? Why will you linger till it is late to receive pardon and till death has shut the door of mercy, till your weeping and wailing will amount to nothing before God?

"Seek ye the Lord while he may be found, call ye upon him while he is near: let the wicked forsake his way, and the unrighteous man his thoughts: and let him return unto the Lord, and he will have mercy upon him; and to our God, for he will abundantly pardon." Isaiah 55:6, 7.

CHAPTER 10

THE DELIVERER OF JACOB AND THE TRIBULATION SAINTS

And so all Israel shall be saved: as it is written, there shall come out of Sion the Deliverer, and shall turn away ungodliness from Jacob, Romans 11:26, After this I beheld, and, lo, a great multitude, which no man could number, of all nations, and kindreds, and people, and tongues, stood before the throne, and before the Lamb, clothed with white robes, and palms in their hands; And cried with a loud voice, saying, Salvation to our God which sitteth upon the throne, and unto the Lamb. And one of the elders answered, saying unto me, What are these which are arrayed in white robes? and whence came they? And I said unto him, Sir, thou knowest. And he said to me, These are they which came out of great tribulation, and have

washed their robes, and made them white in the blood of the Lamb. Therefore are they before the throne of God, and serve him day and night in his temple: and he that sitteth on the throne shall dwell among them. They shall hunger no more, neither thirst any more; neither shall the sun light on them, nor any heat. For the Lamb which is in the midst of the throne shall feed them, and shall lead them unto living fountains of waters: and God shall wipe away all tears from their eyes. Revelation 7:9, 10, 13-17.

The rapture of the saints marks the beginning of a catastrophic and disastrous seven years of great tribulation on earth. It will take place simultaneously with the marriage supper of the Lamb. While the saints will be in an unspeakable joy in the glamour of a glorious marriage supper of the Lamb and in the judgement seat of Christ for reward, those that are left behind will be subject to a shameful torture and molestation. It is the period of God's fiery wrath and that of the antichrist. They are years of devastating woe.

SDuring this time, Satan will set up his government on earth through the antichrist. He will claim ownership of all things and will proclaim himself as God. He will cause fire to fall from heaven and perform many miracles to deceive people. All people from every tribe and nation of the world, both great and small, will be made to worship him and to receive a mark of his name 666 on their forehead or at the back of their right hand.

And they worshipped the dragon which gave power unto the beast: and they

worshipped the beast, saying, Who is like unto the beast? Who is able to make war with him? And there was given unto him a mouth speaking great things and blasphemies; and power was given unto him to continue forty and two months. And he opened his mouth in blasphemy against God, to blaspheme his name, and his tabernacle, and them that dwell in heaven. And it was given unto him to make war with the saints, and to overcome them: and power was given him over all kindreds, and tongues, and nations.

And all that dwell upon the earth shall worship him, whose names are not written in the book of life of the Lamb slain from the foundation of the world. And he doeth great wonders, so that he maketh fire come down from heaven on the earth in the sight of men, And deceiveth them that dwell on the earth by the means of those miracles which

he had power to do in the sight of the beast; saying to them that dwell on the earth, that they should make an image to the beast, which had the wound by a sword, and did live. And he had power to give life unto the image of the beast, that the image of the beast should both speak, and cause that as many as would not worship the image of the beast should be killed. And he causeth all, both small and great, rich and poor, free and bond, to receive a mark in their right hand, or in their foreheads: And that no man might buy or sell, save he that had the mark, or the name of the beast, or the number of his name. Here is wisdom. Let him that hath understanding count the number of the beast: for it is the number of a man; and his number is Six hundred threescore and six. Revelation 13:4-8; 13-18.

He will make war with the saints (Tribulation saints both the Gentiles and

Israel) and will overcome them. It is going to be a terrible moment of affliction for all that may attempt to refuse the mark.

When Jesus was describing the torture and the tribulation of this time, He said,

For then shall be great tribulation such as was not since the beginning of the world to this time, no, nor ever shall be. Matthew 24:21.

Do you note the word of our Lord that it would be a great tribulation such as was not since God created the heaven and the earth, and that after that, such terrible time will not be found again? I have read many terrible tortures in the past. There were some of them that were beaten, and stoned till they died. Some of them were killed by sword and some with a saw and another fried in hot oil. Some were crucified while others were given to wild animals to destroy. Yet, Jesus said it is such tribulation that has never been.

I have read of people that were put on a rack in excruciating pain for the sake of their faith. Some were tied down alive and had their foreskin removed slowly with hot water till they either died or denied their faith. Many have been burnt alive and many have their fingernails removed by force, one after the other till they die or deny their faith.

Here are some of the horrible torture in the past from the Foxe's book of martyrs by John Foxe

1. **Polycarp** - After feeding the guards that arrested him, he asked for an hour of prayer. Though the guards were sorry, they still had to act in order to kill him. The fire that

burned from the dry sticks encircled him, but did not touch him. Then, they pierced him with a sword right in the midst of the fire and he died.

2. **Perpetua** - She was made to run between men set in two rows and was severely lashed. She was offered freedom if she would sacrifice an idol. Her nursing baby was taken from her and into prison with Felicitas. They were made naked and put in a net for animals to gore.

Juliana was arrested for being a Christian, put in a bag with several snakes and scorpions and later thrown to the sea.

3. **Nichomachus** placed on a rack but couldn't endure, fell on the rack and died "unhappy wretch, why

will you buy a moment of ease at the expense of a miserable eternity", Denisa. She was beheaded for saying this.

4. **Agatha** - Christian lady known for piety and remarkable beauty. She refused the advances of governor quintain who handed her over to a woman running a brothel. While she maintained her faith, she was scourged, torn with sharp hooks and placed upon a live coal on a broken glass.

5. **Timothy of Mauritania** - Arrested after a few weeks' wedding for being in charge of the bible Arrianus, the governor asked him to bring the bible for burning. Who answered "if I had children, I would sooner turn them over to go to be sacrificed than I would the word of

God".

Hearing this, commanded his two eyes to be removed with red hot iron standing on his feet with a stone tied to his neck. His wife who persuaded him to deny his faith was charged with mistaken love, so she followed and both of them were tortured and crucified. Jesus is saying, whatever tribulation you have read about or seen in life cannot be compared with the great tribulation that will transpire on earth after the rapture.

I pray you will not be a victim. However, in case you miss the rapture and are privileged not to die in the process, you still have hope to make God's kingdom and to reign with Christ for a thousand years. Though the time of great tribulation is meant to prepare the nation Israel for her Messiah, all Gentiles that will not submit to the deceptive government of the antichrist will also be saved as tribulation saints.

As many that will not serve him nor take his mark 666 will be exposed to unimaginable torture. As many that can endure it till death will be saved as tribulation saints. They shall reign with Christ forever more. Meanwhile, the antichrist will restore daily sacrifice and will make a covenant with Israel for one week (that is the seven years of great tribulation) and will break the covenant in the middle of the week.

And he shall confirm the covenant with many for one week: and in the midst of the week he shall cause the sacrifice and the oblation to cease, and for the overspreading of abominations he shall make it desolate, even until the consummation, and that determined shall be poured upon the desolate. Daniel 9: 27.

Yea, he magnified himself even to the prince of the host, and by him the daily sacrifice was taken away, and the place of his sanctuary was cast down. And an host was given him against the daily sacrifice by reason of transgression, and it cast down the truth to the ground; and it practised, and prospered. Then I heard one saint speaking, and another saint said unto that certain saint which spake, How long shall be the vision concerning the daily sacrifice, and

the transgression of desolation, to give both the sanctuary and the host to be trodden under foot? Daniel 8:11-13.

When ye therefore shall see the abomination of desolation, spoken of by Daniel the prophet, stand in the holy place, who so readeth, let him understand. Matthew 24:15.

At this juncture, the Israelites will take their stand against sin and will refuse to bow to the government of antichrist.

The remnant of Israel shall not do iniquity, nor speak lies; neither shall a deceitful tongue be found in their mouth: for they shall feed and lie down, and none shall make them afraid. Zephaniah 3:13.

And so all Israel shall be saved: as it is written, There shall come out of Sion

the Deliverer, and shall turn away ungodliness from Jacob. Romans 11:26.

For **'there shall come out of Sion a deliverer and shall turn away ungodliness from Jacob.**

Jesus is our Deliverer sent to turn away every form of ungodliness and sins that could easily beset you. That is what He came for. He knew you cannot deliver yourself. Why will you wait till the agony of the great tribulation? Yield yourself to Him and He will deliver you completely.

At last, all the saints that will be saved through the rapture, the tribulation saints and the Old and New Testament saints shall come to mount Zion, the city of our God and the general assembly of the heroes of faith we read about. What a day of joy it will be to see our loving and crucified Saviour face to face and to meet with the saints that have gone before us. Then shall be fulfilled the word of God.

But ye are come unto mount Sion, and unto the city of the living God, the heavenly Jerusalem, and to an innumerable company of angels, To the general assembly and church of the firstborn, which are written in heaven, and to God the Judge of all, and to the spirits of just men made perfect. Hebrews 12:22, 23.

The joy of this great assembly of the saints is expressed in the song of a Progenitor, E.E. Hewitt (1898);

Sing the wondrous love of Jesus, Sing his mercy and his grace,

In the mansions bright and blessed, Hell

prepares for us a place.

Refrain:

When we all get to heaven
What a day of rejoicing
that will be! When we all
see Jesus,
Well sing and shout the
victory.

While we walk the
pilgrim pathway,
Clouds will overspread
the sky,
But when travelling
days are over, Not a
shadow, not a sigh.

Let us then be true
and faithful, Trusting,
serving every day,
Just one glimpse of
Him in glory, Will the

toils of Life repay.

the very God of peace sanctify you wholly; and I pray God your whole spirit and soul and body be preserved blameless unto the coming of our Lord Jesus Christ.
1 Thessalonians 5:23. Amen.
See you there by the grace of God at the first flight of the saints to the marriage supper of the Lamb. Remain rapturable.

MARANATHA

For More Enquiry and Copies of this Book,

Contact:

The Way of Truth Mission.

Kabba: 08032200580, 08027575214, 08065094454

Lagos: 08027575137, 08127800460

Ekiti: 08036316536, 07035740860

Lokoja: 08027575135,

E-mail:

thewayoftruthmission@gmail.com

www.ingramcontent.com/pod-product-compliance
Lightning Source LLC
LaVergne TN
LVHW010600160826
845677LV00013B/3193